Sous Vide Cookbook

Complete Cookbook Using Modern and Simple Recipes Cooking Under Vacuum

Laura Miller

Table of Contents

Introduction 7

Chapter 1: The Basics Of Sous Vide 8
What is Sous Vide Cooking! 8
The basic history of Sous Vide 9

Chapter 2: The benefits of Sous Vide Cooking 10

Chapter 3: Setting up your Sous Vide Kitchen 12
The main device 12
Extra essentials 14

Chapter 4: The Basic Sous Vide Cooking Method 16
Sous Vide cooking process made easy. 16
The sealing methods 18

Chapter 5: Breakfast Recipes 19
Exclusive Scrambled Eggs 19
Devilled Eggs Nicoise 21
Garlic Parmesan Broccolini 22
Manhattan Pastrami Scramble 23
Elegant Squash Casserole 24
Earyly Morning Sous Vide Quinoa 26
Bar-Style Pink Pickled Eggs 27

Chapter 6: Poultry Recipes 29
Authentic Poached Chicken 29
Chicken Cacciatore 31
Duck a la Orange 32
Turkey Burgers 34
Duck Breast with Balsamic Fig Jam 35
Mirin Teriyaki Wings.. 36
Chicken Marsala.. 38
Homely Moroccan Chicken Dish.. 40
Simple Panko Crusted Chicken... 42
Juicy Adobo Chicken.. 44
Amazing Sweet Chili Chicken 45

Chapter 7: Fish and Seafood Recipes 47
Hearty Shrimp Salad... 47
Scallops And Citrus Sauce 49
Salmon With Yogurt and Dill Sauce 51
Simple Clam Sauce And Linguine 52
Secret Swordfish Picatta Dish... 54
Generous Shrimp Scamp 55
Fancy Bacon And Sole Fish... 57
Wholesome Red Snapper.. 58
Juicy Coriander And Garlic Squid Delight................................ 59

Chapter 8: Beef Recipes 61
Juicy Spiced Ribs 61
Authentic BBQ Beef Brisket 63
Exquisite Beef Tri-Tip 64
Juicy Corned Beef 65
The Easy Beef Wellington 66
Mazing Prime Rib 68
Grandermother's Beef Brisket 70

Chapter 9: Potato Recipes 72
Amazing Potato Confit 72
Garlic And Rosemary Potato Mash 73
Potato Salad 74
Creamy Potato Mash 76
Mini Fingerling Potatoes 77
Sweet Potatoes And Pecans 78
Delicious Candied Potatoes 79

Chapter 10: Fruits and Vegetables Recipes 81
Tasty Hazelnut Green Beans 81
Hearty Pear And Walnut Salad 83
Juicy Shallot And Cream Peas 85
Exquisite Sous Vide Cactus 86
Momofuku Clear Brussels 87
Sensational Onion Julienne 89
Delicious Butter Radish 90

Thyme Lard Broad Beans 91

Sous Vide Vegetable and Fruit Recipes 92

Chapter 11: Dessert Recipes 94

Sassy Peach Cobbler 94

Curried Acorn Squash 96

Smoked Salmon Eggs Benedict 97

Salty Custard 98

Pears In Pomegranate Juice 100

Blueberry Lime Compote 101

Tropical Pineapple 102

Orange Compote 103

Pumpkin Crème Bruele 104

Conclusion 106

Introduction

There is a burning desire inside all of us to be able to create beautiful meals with ease! Sadly though, not all of us blessed with the innate natural talent of cooking! Or, perhaps even we know that we can cook, our busy schedule often seems to hinder our progress and prevent us from being able to give enough time to the kitchen to prepare a hearty meal. But that does that we should let go of our culinary dreams? Of course not! The Sous Vide cooking devices are here to change just that! As you will see after going through the book, Sous Vide cooking devices have the capacity to create restaurant quality gourmet meals right at home! And the best part is that you won't even have to be a Masterchef to do that! Interesting right? Believe me; Sous Vide is going to blow your mind! Even though the concept of Sous Vide cooking gained a right amount of traction as of late, there are still a large number of people who are unfamiliar with the concept. If you happen to be one of them, then you are in luck! The core aim of this book is to only provide you with a bunch of delicious and mouthwatering recipes, but also to act as a basic beginner's guide to help you familiarize yourself with the fundamentals. If you already know what there is to know about Sous Vide cooking, feel free to skip the intro and jump right into the recipes! But I would still encourage you to take a little bit of your time to skim through the following pages. Who knows, even if you are an expert, you might get to know something new! I hope that you enjoy your Sous Vide cooking experience! Bon Appetit.!

Chapter 1: The Basics Of Sous Vide

So, without any more delays, let me start off with the most fundamental question first!

What is Sous Vide Cooking!

Unlike the names of many other cooking appliances that tend to refer to the name of the appliance itself, Instant Pot for example! The term "Sous Vide" actually refers to the cooking process itself! But a literal meaning of the word "Sous Vide" would be "Under Vacuum," which comes from the French Vocabulary. And this is again linked to the cooking method itself! As one of the main difference between regular cooking and Sous Vide cooking is the fact that you are required to seal your ingredients inside an Air Tight zip bag and cook it under precisely heated water bath. And just in case you are wondering, this is where the Sous Vide device comes into play! The primary function of the Sous Vide Immersion Circulator is to heat up your water bath to an exact temperature and hold the temperature for the whole cooking period. This extreme temperature control allows you to cook fantastic gourmet quality meals with ease seamlessly. There was a time when Sous Vide was considered to be a luxury and was only used in exquisite TV shows such as Iron Chef or Masterchef, or by world-renowned chefs in 5-star restaurants! However, with the development of culinary technologies, Sous Vide devices have now become more affordable than ever! Sous Vide is now readily available for the standard mass to utilize and cook restaurant quality gourmet dishes in no time! So, even if you are not a culinary savant, with the help of Sous Vide, you will still be able to prepare meals that boast spot on flavors and textures. We will go deeper into what you are going to need for Sous Vide cooking and how you can prepare your kitchen! But before that, let me give you a little history lesson and give you an idea of the origin of Sous Vide cooking.

The basic history of Sous Vide

If you are a foodie like me, then you most definitely tend to explore a wide variety of restaurants to try out various tasty dishes. Trust me when I say this, that you have almost definitely had the privilege of experiencing Sous Vide prepared meals, even without you knowing it! This is a technique that has been used in top class restaurants all around the world to take their meals to the next level! Believe it or not, though, there's no "Super Secret" behind this manner of cooking! At the heart of the process, lies a very fundamental matter of being able to keep the water bath heated at a steady temperature consistently. This extreme control over the cooking temperature allows even novice chefs to prepare excellent meals with minimal effort. And if you think that this high-tech device is a very recent creation, then you are slightly misguided my friend! While the modern devices are the creation of advance culinary sciences, the actual origin of the Sous Vide technique dates back to mid-1970s. That was the era when a back then famous chef known as Georges Paulus tried to develop a cooking method that would allow people to minimize the cost making the extremely rich foie gras. His advanced technique was, later on, picked up Chef Bruno Goussault who further enhanced the technique and started to cater the passengers off first-class Air Lines. The passengers were hypnotized entirely by the quality and flavor of the meals! After Bruno and after two decades of seamless innovation, the technique of Sous Vide has now spread all over the world and has garnered a reputation of being one of the "Best' cooking techniques out there!

Chapter 2: The benefits of Sous Vide Cooking

Sous Vide cooking is not just about cooking excellent meals with ease! It also comes with a good chunk of benefits as well!

While there are lots of benefits of using Sous Vide, below are some of the most crucial ones that you should know about!

- One of the most apparent and excellent benefits of Sous Vide cooking is the simplicity involved with the cooking process. Even though some people consider Sous Vide is cooking to be somewhat confusing, the truth is far from! The beginning of the process takes a little bit of effort as you are going to have to prepare the ingredients, however, once you have prepared your ingredients, the rest is easy! The Sous Vide cooker takes care of the rest.
- Sous Vide cooking allows the moisture of your meals to be retained correctly! This helps to enhance the flavor of your meal, thanks to the presence of added and more intense cooking juice. It helps to bring out the flavors of your dish considerably.
- Sous Vide cooking doesn't require you to add any unnecessary fat or oil while cooking, so right off the bat! Your prepared meal will be extremely healthy. This allows your body to lower your body's cholesterol level slowly and improves your health in the long run.
- Meals that are prepared using the Sous Method are more comfortable to digest and puts less strain on your body and gut.
- Often, exposing the meal ingredients to direct heat, air or water causes them to lose a significant amount of nutrition. The Sous Vide method requires you to seal your ingredients in an Air Tight pouch, which means that there is no way that your meal with coming in contact with air, direct heat or even water! Ultimately what happens is that your nutrients will stay perfectly intact!

- Sous Vide cooked meals are known for their tenderness when compared to other cooking methods. This happens because the food never gets hotter than the water, which is itself at a shallow temperature throughout the process. The tenderness of the meat is retained entirely in the process as meat cells don't burst during cooking and the collagen located in the tissue of the meat do not get broken down.
- And perhaps more importantly, it will prevent your expensive cuts from being under/overcooked and save you a bucket load of money!

Chapter 3: Setting up your Sous Vide Kitchen

I am sure that after knowing about the amazing benefits of the diet! You must be very eager to start cooking right away! However, I would like you to take a step back and know the basics of how you can prepare your kitchen.

The main device

The heart of your Sous Vide kitchen will be your Sous Vide device! So, let's talk about that first. Now, you should know that there are mainly two different types of Sous Vide methods that you can utilize at home. Sous Vide Ovens and Sous Vide c Immersion Circulators. Even though the primary objective of both of these is the same, they still have some minute differences. Let me break both of them for you to make your choice easier.

Sous Vide Ovens

Sous Vide Ovens are perhaps the easiest way to start off your Sous Vide journey. Each of the All-Inclusive Sous Vide Oven comes with a reservoir, designed explicitly for Sous Vide Cooking alongside the heating device. These ovens also come with timers, digital thermometers, and even vacuum sealers! The look pretty sleek, and if you can afford an expensive one, you might even get the option of searing your dish built-in! But, as you can already guess, these appliances are pretty expensive, so that is something you should consider.

Immersion Circulators

On the other hand, Sous Vide immersion Circulators are excellent for their efficiency. They get the job done and don't cost as much either! For novice chefs and individuals who want to experiment with the booking form, these are the ones to go for! At the time of writing, some of the more attractive ones were as follows:

- **Anova Wifi Precision Cooker:** This is possibly the ultimate Sous Vide cooker out there, and it took the world by storm when it came out! Asides from extremely actual cooking, Anova devices are well known for their Bluetooth and Wi-Fi functionalities that allows users to control their device from afar.

  At the time of writing, the lowest market price was 109$

- **ChefSteps Joule:** ChefSteps has mainly been known to be the pioneer of the "Smart Kitchen" scene, and when they stepped into the market with their first sous vide machine, The ChefSteps Joule, jaws dropped!

  The device has a fantastic design and a very compact size, but packs the same level of power that can rival any Sous Vide device of double its size!

  This is the prime example of "Big Things Comes in Smaller Packages."

  At the time of writing, the lowest market price was 199$

- **Sansaire:** Sansaire devices are pretty unique regarding their outlook. They are possibly the most attractive cookers available in the market! And that beautiful aesthetic comes packed with a cooking device that can accurately heat up water to the smallest temperature of 0.1 degrees. The device is compact and does not that that much space either.

  At the time of writing, the lowest market price was 166$

Extra essentials

Once you have decided which Sous Vide device you are going to purchase, the next step for you would acquire some of the necessary equipment needed for Sous Vide cooking.

Non-Stick Pan And Cast Iron Skillet

I have mentioned this earlier, that some recipes might require you to add some finishing touches in order to amplify their flavors further. For this, searing of the dish might be required! Therefore, it is essential that you keep a good quality skillet or non-stick pan nearby so that you can do the job quickly.

Saucepan

Some recipes might even call for a saucepan to prepare an extra sauce for the dish. So, keeping a saucepan in your kitchen won't hurt!

Re-sealable Zip Bags and Mason Jars

For zip bags, standard heavy duty zip bags are fantastic as they can easily withstand high temperatures of 195 degrees Fahrenheit with ease.

And to clarify,

Sous Vide does not "Strictly" require you to purchase an overly expensive vacuum sealing machine to zip up the lock bags properly! Yes, expensive machines will make your life a little bit easier, but if you are on a tight budget you can as quickly achieve excellent results using a simple "Water Immersion/Displacement" method! (Discussed below) Before buying the bags, always ensure that the bags are "Freezer Safe" and have a double seal. For jars, you can go for glass canning jars or mason jars with a tight lid.

Sizeable Sized Container For Water Bath

The container is where you will prepare your water bath, so it is wise to go for a reasonably large container. A standard 8-12 quart stock pot would do the trick as well! But if you want to go big, then go for the 12-quart square polycarbonate food storage containers. Regardless of which container you choose, make sure to check if the container can be heated up to 203 degrees Fahrenheit.

Vacuum Sealers

This is the only equipment on this list that you may consider to be optional. Vacuum sealers are appliances that are designed for just one purpose, and that is to seal your zip bags by sucking out the air from the inside. It is a matter of cash vs. effort here! You can seal your zip bags by using the immersion method, but if can ditch some extra dollars, then going for a Vacuum sealer isn't such a bad idea.

Chapter 4: The Basic Sous Vide Cooking Method

Contrary to popular belief, Sous Vide cooking isn't that difficult at all! Now that you know the basics and required equipment of the Sous Vide let me walk you through the basics of Sous Vide cooking in just a few easy steps.

Sous Vide cooking process made easy.

All the recipes found in this book will be a variation of the steps you will find below.

- The first step of any Sous Vide recipe is to prepare your water bath. So, once you have decided which container you are going to use as your water bath. Fill it up with sufficient amount of water and dip your immersion circulator. Set up the heat and time, and let it heat up.
- While the water bath heats up to your desired temperature, you should prepare your ingredients accordingly. Different recipes might call for a different preparation method, so ready them accordingly. Oil them, spice them as needed to enhance the flavors.
- Once you have prepared your ingredient, the next step for you would be to seal your ingredient inside a vacuum sealed zip bag. Now, there are many ways of doing this, but throughout our book, we will be following a very method known as the "immersion method" or "water displacement" method. The method has been described below for your convenience as well.
- Some recipes might ask you to transfer your ingredients to a Mason Jar and submerge them underwater to cook them. The method for sealing Mason Jars is also described below.

- If you don't want to go through the hassle of sealing the ingredients manually, then you can always opt for Vacuum Sealer Machines! These are appliances that are purposely designed for sucking out the air from Zip bags and sealing them with ease. These devices were pretty expensive once, but you can get them for a relatively low price these days.
- So, once you have sealed your meal following your desired method, next you are to submerge them underwater and let them cook for the desired amount of time.
- Now, you can eat your meal right now! But most recipes will ask you to follow some finishing steps like searing the meal for a few seconds to further enrich the texture and flavors of the dish.

And that's pretty much it!

The sealing methods

As mentioned above, the following are the sealing methods that you should know of.

Water Displacement/Immersion Method: This is the method that we are going to use the most in the book! The necessary procedure is to place the bag with the food in a water bath about half to two thirds way down. Once you have done that, you will soon realize that the air is gradually leaving from the bag. Once all the air has left the bag, fold the ends or seal the bag. That's it!

Finger Tip Tight: This is the method that you are going to need

The thing to remember when tightening a jar for Sous Vide is that, whenever you are submerging the jar underwater, the tightness of the lid should be loose enough so that it allows air to escape from the jar. The simplest way to do that is always to start to tighten your jar usually and stop at right where you start to feel resistance from the jar.

Chamber Sealing Method: This method is essential when you will want to use vacuum sealers. It allows you to seal more than one bag and has a wide surface area. Personally, though, I don't prefer to use Vacuum Sealers for home, as even though they don't cost much, they are still an extra burden to bear. With the Immersion method, you can very easily seal your meals, free of cost!

And with that, you are now ready to dive into the fantastic Sous Vide recipes!

Chapter 5: Breakfast Recipes

Exclusive Scrambled Eggs

SERVING: 4

PREP TIME: 5 MINUTES

COOK TIME: 40 MINUTES

INGREDIENTS

- 8 large whole eggs
- ½ cup medium cheddar cheese, grated
- 4 tablespoons heavy cream
- 4 tablespoons 2% milk
- Pinch of salt
- 2 tablespoons butter
- Finely chopped fresh chives

HOW TO

1. Prepare your water bath by submerging your Sous Vide immersion circulator and raise the temperature to 170 degree F
2. Take a bowl and whisk in eggs, cheese, cream, milk, salt and mix well
3. Transfer the mix to a Sous Vide zip bag and seal using immersion method
4. Transfer bag to water bath and cook for 20 minutes
5. Remove bag and lay it on a smooth surface, gently massage to ensure the egg mix is cooked evenly
6. Return bag to water bath and cook for 20 minutes more
7. Remove egg and pour into serving dish
8. Top with chives and enjoy!

NUTRITION VALUES (PER SERVING)

- Calories: 91
- Fat: 7g
- Carbohydrates: 1g
- Protein: 1g

Devilled Eggs Nicoise

SERVING: 6

PREP TIME: 30 MINUTES

COOK TIME: 1 HOUR

INGREDIENTS

- 6 large eggs
- 1 tablespoon sesame oil
- 2 tablespoons black olives, minced
- 1 small tomato, seeded and minced
- Juice of 1 lemon
- 1 tablespoon plain Greek yogurt
- 1 tablespoon Dijon mustard
- 2 tablespoon fresh parsley, minced, additional for garnish

HOW TO

1. Prepare your water bath by submerging your Sous Vide immersion circulator and raise the temperature to 170 degree F
2. Transfer eggs to a Sous Vide zip bag and seal using immersion method
3. Submerge underwater and cook for 1 hour
4. Take a bowl of cold water and let eggs cold
5. Peel carefully, then cut each egg in half lengthwise
6. Take another bowl to scoop egg yolks into a bowl.
7. Stir in tomato, lemon, mustard, olive, oil, parsley and yogurt
8. Spoon egg whites with the egg yolk mixture
9. Garnish with parsley
10. Serve and enjoy!

NUTRITION VALUES (PER SERVING)

- Calories: 160
- Fat: 12.38g
- Carbohydrates: 2.59g
- Protein: 9.33g

Garlic Parmesan Broccolini

SERVING: 4

PREP TIME: 10 MINUTES

COOK TIME: 30 MINUTES

INGREDIENTS

- 1 bunch broccolini, washed and trimmed
- ¼ teaspoon salt
- 1 clove garlic, crushed
- 2 tablespoons Parmesan, grated
- 1 tablespoon butter
- ¼ teaspoon pepper

HOW TO

1. Prepare your water bath by submerging your Sous Vide immersion circulator and raise the temperature to 185 degree
2. Transfer all ingredients except Parmesan cheese to a Sous Vide zip bag and seal using immersion method
3. Cook for 30 minutes
4. Once done, remove the bag from water bath
5. Sprinkle with parmesan
6. Serve and enjoy!

NUTRITION VALUES (PER SERVING)

- Calories: 62
- Fat: 3.57g
- Carbohydrates: 4.75g
- Protein: 4.73g

Manhattan Pastrami Scramble

Serving: 3

Prep Time: 10 minutes

Cook Time: 15 minutes

INGREDIENTS

- 6 large eggs
- 2 tablespoons heavy cream
- 2 tablespoons butter, melted
- ¼ teaspoon salt
- 3 slices buttered rye toast, for serving
- ½ teaspoon pepper
- ½ cup thick cut pastrami, shredded

HOW TO

1. Prepare your water bath by submerging your Sous Vide immersion circulator and raise the temperature to 167 degree F
2. Take a bowl and whisk together eggs, butter, salt, cream and pepper
3. Stir in pastrami
4. Pour the egg mixture and transfer to a Sous Vide zip bag and seal using immersion method
5. Submerge underwater and cook for 15 minutes
6. Gently massage for 3 to 5 minutes to make scramble
7. Serve pastrami scramble with rye toast
8. Enjoy!

NUTRITION VALUES (PER SERVING)

- Calories: 287
- Fat: 21.28g
- Carbohydrates: 12.76g
- Protein: 11.3g

Elegant Squash Casserole

SERVING: 4

PREP TIME: 30 MINUTES

COOK TIME: 1 HOUR

INGREDIENTS

- 2 tablespoons unsalted butter
- ¾ cup onion, chopped
- 1 and ½ pounds zucchini, quartered lengthwise, and sliced into ¼ inch thick pieces
- Salt and pepper to taste
- ½ cup whole milk
- 2 large whole eggs
- ½ cup crumbled plain potato chips

HOW TO

1. Prepare your water bath by submerging your Sous Vide immersion circulator and raise the temperature to 176 degree F
2. Take a 4 by 1 pint canning jar and grease well
3. Take a large skillet and place it over medium heat
4. Add butter and let it melt
5. Add onions and Saute for 7 minutes
6. Add zucchini and season with salt
7. Saute for 10 minutes and season with more salt and pepper
8. Divide the zucchini mix into greased jars and let them cool
9. Take a bowl and whisk in milk, salt and eggs
10. Grind some pepper on top
11. Divide mix amongst jar and loosely close the lid
12. Submerge and cook for 60 minutes
13. Let it cool for 5 minutes and serve over potato chips
14. Enjoy!

NUTRITION VALUES (PER SERVING)

- Calories: 319
- Fat: 19g
- Carbohydrates: 29g
- Protein: 10g

Earyly Morning Sous Vide Quinoa

SERVING: 2

PREP TIME: 5 MINUTES

COOK TIME: 3 HOURS

INGREDIENTS

- ½ cup whole grain quinoa
- ¾ cup warm water
- ½ teaspoon kosher salt

HOW TO

1. Prepare your water bath by submerging your Sous Vide immersion circulator and raise the temperature to 180 degree F
2. Add quinoa, ¾ cup warm water in a mason jar
3. Stir in salt and gently lock the jar to ensure it is not fully tightened
4. Submerge and let it cook for 3 hours
5. Once done, take the jar out and let it cool
6. Open lid and add your desired mix-ins such as almonds, berries etc.
7. Serve and enjoy!

NUTRITION VALUES (PER SERVING)

- Calories: 280
- Fat: 3g
- Carbohydrates: 25g
- Protein: 7g

Bar-Style Pink Pickled Eggs

SERVING: 6

PREP TIME: 20 MINUTES

COOK TIME: 2 HOURS

INGREDIENTS

- 6 eggs
- 1 tablespoon whole peppercorn
- 1 bay leaf
- ½ tablespoon salt
- 2 cloves garlic
- ¼ cup sugar
- 1 cup white vinegar
- Juice from 1 can beets

HOW TO

1. Prepare your water bath by submerging your Sous Vide immersion circulator and raise the temperature to 170 degree F
2. Transfer eggs to a Sous Vide zip bag and seal using immersion method
3. Submerge underwater and cook for 1 hour
4. Take a bowl of cold water and let eggs cold and peel carefully
5. In the bag in which you cooked the eggs, add with vinegar, sugar, garlic, beet juice, salt and bay leaf
6. Transfer eggs back to the bag
7. Transfer to water bath and cook for additional 1 hour
8. Once done, remove the bag from water bath
9. Move eggs with pickling liquid to the refrigerator and cool completely
10. Serve and enjoy!

NUTRITION VALUES (PER SERVING)

- Calories: 166
- Fat: 10.08g
- Carbohydrates: 7.34g
- Protein: 9.3g

Chapter 6: Poultry Recipes

Authentic Poached Chicken

SERVING: 4

PREP TIME: 45 MINUTES

COOK TIME: 6 HOURS

INGREDIENTS

- 1 whole bone-in, chicken, trussed
- 1 quart low sodium chicken stock
- 2 tablespoons soy sauce
- 5 sprigs fresh thyme
- 2 dried bay leaves
- 2 cups carrots, thickly sliced
- ½ ounces dried mushrooms
- 3 tablespoons unsalted butter

HOW TO

1. Prepare your water bath by submerging your Sous Vide immersion circulator and raise the temperature to 150 degree F
2. Add soy sauce, chicken, stock, herbs, vegetables to a heavy duty Sous Vide zip bag
3. Seal using immersion method
4. Submerge and cook for 6 hours
5. Remove chicken and strain vegetables
6. Pat them dry and season with chicken and veggies with olive oil, salt and pepper
7. Pre-heat your oven to 450 degree F
8. Transfer chicken and veggies to baking sheet and bake for 10 minutes
9. Take a large saucepan and place it over low heat
10. Add cooking liquid from the bag and simmer
11. Remove from heat and whisk in butter, dissolve
12. Carve the chicken and discard skin
13. Season with salt and peppper

14. Divide veggies, chicken between platters and serve with sauce
15. Enjoy!

NUTRITION VALUES (PER SERVING)

- Calories: 435
- Fat: 26g
- Carbohydrates: 17g
- Protein: 34g

Chicken Cacciatore

SERVING: 4

PREP TIME: 20 MINUTES

COOK TIME: 3 HOURS

INGREDIENTS

- 4 boneless, skinless chicken breast
- 14 ounces whole tomatoes, crushed
- 1 red bell pepper, cut into strips
- 1 bay leaf
- 1 teaspoon salt
- 1 small onion, sliced
- 2 springs fresh thyme
- 1 teaspoon pepper to cooking for pasta serving
- 3 clove garlic, minced

HOW TO

1. Prepare your water bath by submerging your Sous Vide immersion circulator and raise the temperature to 145 degree F
2. Transfer tomatoes, onion, chicken, bell pepper, bay leaf, garlic, thyme, salt and pepper to a Sous Vide zip bag and seal using immersion method
3. Submerge underwater and cook for 3 hours
4. Once done, remove the bag from water bath
5. Serve and enjoy!

NUTRITION VALUES (PER SERVING)

- Calories: 336
- Fat: 6.87g
- Carbohydrates: 11.28g
- Protein: 65.42g

Duck a la Orange

SERVING: 2

PREP TIME: 20 MINUTES

COOK TIME: 2 HOURS AND 30 MINUTES

INGREDIENTS

- 1 orange, sliced
- 1 shallot, chopped
- 2 and ½ ounces duck breast fillets, skin on
- 4 cloves garlic
- 4 springs thyme
- 1 tablespoon sherry vinegar
- 1 teaspoon black peppercorns
- 2 tablespoons butter
- Salt, to taste
- ¼ cup red wine

HOW TO

1. Prepare your water bath by submerging your Sous Vide immersion circulator and raise the temperature to 135 degree F
2. Top the breast with orange slices, garlic, peppercorns, shallot and thyme
3. Transfer the duck breast fillets to a Sous Vide zip bags and seal using immersion method
4. Submerge underwater and cook for 2hours and 30 minutes
5. Once done, remove the breast
6. Take a large skillet and heat it over medium-high heat
7. Sear the duck, keeping skin side down for 30 seconds and place the breast aside and keep warm
8. Add sherry and vinegar and wine in the same skillet
9. Transfer cooking liquid from bag to the skillet and bring to simmer, simmer for 5 minutes
10. Stir in the butter and simmer for 1 minute
11. Once cooled transfer into a food processor
12. Serve the duck with prepared sauce and enjoy!

NUTRITION VALUES (PER SERVING)

- Calories: 466
- Fat: 27.4g
- Carbohydrates: 15.1g
- Protein: 34.5g

Turkey Burgers

SERVING: 6

PREP TIME: 20 MINUTES + INACTIVE TIME

COOK TIME: 1 HOUR

INGREDIENTS

- 2 pounds ground lean turkey
- 1 shallot, chopped
- ½ cup sun-dried tomatoes, packed in oil, chopped
- 4 cloves garlic, minced
- ½ cup parsley, chopped
- 1 teaspoon paprika powder
- 1 teaspoon dry mustard powder
- Salt and pepper, to taste

HOW TO

1. Prepare your water bath by submerging your Sous Vide immersion circulator and raise the temperature to 145 degree F
2. Take in a bowl and combine all ingredients
3. Shape the mixture into 6 patties and arrange the patties on a baking sheet lined with parchment paper
4. Freeze for 4 hours
5. Transfer each patty to a Sous Vide zip bags and seal using immersion method
6. Submerge underwater and cook for 1 hour
7. Once done, remove the bag
8. Take a grill pan and heat it over medium-high heat
9. Sear the patties for 1 minute per side
10. Serve it with fresh salad and enjoy!

NUTRITION VALUES (PER SERVING)

- Calories: 212
- Fat: 9.7g
- Carbohydrates: 1.7g
- Protein: 30.5g

Duck Breast with Balsamic Fig Jam

SERVING: 4

PREP TIME: 30 MINUTES

COOK TIME: 3 HOURS

INGREDIENTS

- 2 boneless duck breast
- 1 teaspoon pepper
- 1 teaspoon salt
- ½ cup raw sugar
- ½ cup water
- 6 ounces figs, dried
- ¼ cup balsamic vinegar

HOW TO

1. Prepare your water bath by submerging your Sous Vide immersion circulator and raise the temperature to 140 degree F
2. Season duck breast with salt and pepper and seal into bags
3. Take a separate bag and combine figs, sugar, vinegar and water
4. Transfer the bags to a Sous Vide zip bags and seal using immersion method
5. Submerge underwater and cook for 3 hours
6. Once done, remove the bags
7. Take a pan and transfer the duck to the pan, skin side down
8. Cook on medium high until skin is crisp
9. Remove to plate and place it skin-side up
10. Take a bowl, pour jam and break up any large fig chunks
11. Serve the duck with jam and enjoy!

NUTRITION VALUES (PER SERVING)

- Calories: 400
- Fat: 13.42
- Carbohydrates: 39.77g
- Protein: 30.5g

Mirin Teriyaki Wings

SERVING: 4

PREP TIME: 10 MINUTES

COOK TIME: 45 MINUTES

INGREDIENTS

- 1 and ½ pounds chicken wings, sliced into flats and drummettes
- 1 tablespoon teriyaki sauce
- ½ teaspoon mirin
- ¼ teaspoon fresh ginger, minced
- 1 teaspoon teriyaki sauce
- Vegetable oil, for frying
- Wasabi for garnish
- Salt and freshly ground black pepper

HOW TO

1. Prepare your water bath by submerging your Sous Vide immersion circulator and raise the temperature to 140 degree F
2. Season chicken wings, lightly with salt and pepper
3. Transfer wings to a Sous Vide zip bags and seal using immersion method
4. Submerge underwater and cook for 45 minutes
5. Meanwhile, take a bowl and prepare the sauce; combine teriyaki sauce, mirin, hoisin sauce and ginger
6. Once done, remove the bag and take the chicken out
7. Take a large pan and pour around 2-inches oil on medium high heat
8. fry the wings for 1-2 minutes and transfer to bowl the with prepared sauce
9. Toss to combine
10. Serve wings with wasabi and enjoy!

NUTRITION VALUES (PER SERVING)

- Calories: 335
- Fat: 12.42
- Carbohydrates: 2.4g
- Protein: 49.8g

Chicken Marsala

SERVING: 2

PREP TIME: 20 MINUTES

COOK TIME: 2 HOURS AND 30 MINUTES

INGREDIENTS

- 2 chicken breast, boneless and skinless
- 1 tablespoon butter
- 1 teaspoon salt
- 1 teaspoon pepper
- 1 pound fresh mushroom, sliced
- ½ tablespoon flour
- 1 cup chicken stock
- 2 cloves garlic, minced
- Cooked pasta for serving
- 1 shallot or ½ onion, diced
- 1 cup Marsala wine

HOW TO

1. Prepare your water bath by submerging your Sous Vide immersion circulator and raise the temperature to 140 degree F
2. Add salt and pepper the chicken breast
3. Transfer chicken breast to a Sous Vide zip bags and seal using immersion method
4. Submerge underwater and cook for 2 hours
5. Meanwhile, when chicken is almost cooked , prepare the sauce
6. Take a pan and melt butter and cook garlic for 30 seconds
7. Add flour and cook until bubbling subsides and then pour in the stock wine
8. Continue cooking until sauce is reduced half, and season to taste with salt and pepper
9. Once done, remove the bag and slice across the grain
10. Stir chicken and mushrooms into sauce and serve over pasta
11. Enjoy!

NUTRITION VALUES (PER SERVING)

- Calories: 556
- Fat: 14.42
- Carbohydrates: 21.19g
- Protein: 64.17g

Homely Moroccan Chicken Dish

SERVING: 2

PREP TIME: 10 MINUTES

COOK TIME: 1 HOUR

INGREDIENTS

- 6 chicken tenderloins
- 4 cups pumpkin, cubed and roasted
- 4 cups rocket tomatoes
- 4 tablespoons almonds, sliced
- Juice of 1 lemon
- 2 tablespoons olive oil
- 4 tablespoons red onion, chopped
- 2 pinch paprika
- 2 pinches turmeric
- 2 pinches cumin
- 2 pinches salt

HOW TO

1. Prepare your water bath by submerging your Sous Vide immersion circulator and raise the temperature to 140 degree F
2. Add spices and chicken to a heavy duty Sous Vide zip bag and coat well
3. Seal using immersion method
4. Submerge and cook for 60 minutes
5. Once done, sear the chicken on a hot skillet (1 minute per side)
6. Take another bowl and add remaining ingredients, mix well
7. Add the chicken to the bowl and toss well
8. Serve!

NUTRITION VALUES (PER SERVING)

- Calories: 261
- Fat: 18g
- Carbohydrates: 6g
- Protein: 19g

Simple Panko Crusted Chicken

SERVING: 4

PREP TIME: 30 MINUTES

COOK TIME: 1 HOUR

INGREDIENTS

- 4 boneless chicken breasts
- 1 cup panko bread crumbs
- 1 pound mushrooms, sliced
- Small bunch thyme
- 2 whole eggs
- Salt and pepper to taste
- Canola oil as needed

HOW TO

1. Prepare your water bath by submerging your Sous Vide immersion circulator and raise the temperature to 150 degree F
2. Season chicken with salt and thyme
3. Transfer breast to a re-sealable zip bag and seal using immersion method
4. Submerge and cook for 60 minutes
5. Take a pan and place it over medium heat
6. Add mushrooms and cook until water evaporates
7. Add 3-4 sprigs of thyme and thyme, season with salt and pepper
8. Remove chicken from zip bag and pat it dry
9. Take another pan and heat up oil over medium heat, add chicken in the panko breadcrumbs (Seasoned with salt and pepper) and fry for 1-2 minutes per side
10. Serve with the mushrooms and cooked veggies
11. Enjoy!

NUTRITION VALUES (PER SERVING)

- Calories: 391
- Fat: 5g
- Carbohydrates: 61g
- Protein: 19g

Juicy Adobo Chicken

SERVING: 2

PREP TIME: 5 MINUTES

COOK TIME: 4 HOURS

INGREDIENTS

- 2 chicken leg quarters
- 6 garlic clove, crushed
- ¼ teaspoon black pepper
- 2 bay leaves
- ¼ cup dark soy sauce
- ¼ cup white vinegar

HOW TO

1. Prepare your water bath by submerging your Sous Vide immersion circulator and raise the temperature to 165 degree F
2. Add chicken legs, seasoning, vinegar, soy sauce, bay leaves and garlic cloves to a heavy duty re-sealable bag and seal using immersion method
3. Submerge and cook for 4 hours
4. Remove chicken legs from bag and sear over medium heat (with oil)
5. Strain the cooking liquid from zip bag and pour to a pan over medium heat
6. Heat until thick
7. Pour the sauce over chicken and serve
8. Enjoy!

NUTRITION VALUES (PER SERVING)

- Calories: 320
- Fat: 14g
- Carbohydrates: 23g
- Protein: 16g

Amazing Sweet Chili Chicken

SERVING: 2

PREP TIME: 30 MINUTES

COOK TIME: 2 HOURS

INGREDIENTS

- 4 chicken thighs
- 2 tablespoons olive oil
- Salt and pepper to taste
- 1 garlic clove, crushed
- 3 tablespoons fish sauce
- ¼ cup lime sauce
- 1 tablespoon palm sugar
- 3 tablespoons Thai basil, chopped
- 3 tablespoons cilantro, chopped
- 2 red chilies, deseeded, chopped
- 1 tablespoon sweet chili sauce

HOW TO

1. Prepare your water bath by submerging your Sous Vide immersion circulator and raise the temperature to 150 degree F
2. Cover chicken thighs with cling film and let it chill for a while
3. Transfer to zip bag alongside olive oil, salt and pepper
4. Seal using immersion method and submerge, cook for 2 hours
5. Once done, take a pan and place it over medium heat
6. Heat up olive oil
7. Chop chicken into 4-5 pieces
8. Cook them in oil until crispy
9. Take a bowl and add the dressing ingredients and mix well
10. Season the fried chicken pieces with salt and serve with the sauce
11. Enjoy!

NUTRITION VALUES (PER SERVING)

- Calories: 721
- Fat: 54g
- Carbohydrates: 9g
- Protein: 46g

Chapter 7: Fish and Seafood Recipes

Hearty Shrimp Salad

SERVING: 2

PREP TIME: 10 MINUTES

COOK TIME: 24 MINUTES

INGREDIENTS

- 1 red onion, chopped
- Juice of 2 limes
- 1 teaspoon extra virgin olive oil
- ¼ teaspoon salt
- 1/8 teaspoon pepper
- 1 pound raw shrimp, peeled and de-veined
- 1 tomato, diced
- 1 avocado, diced
- 1 jalapeno, seeded and diced
- 1 tablespoon cilantro, chopped

HOW TO

1. Prepare your water bath by submerging your Sous Vide immersion circulator and raise the temperature to 148 degree F
2. Add lime juice, red onion, salt, white pepper, extra virgin olive oil, white pepper, shrimp to Sous Vide zip bag
3. Seal using immersion method
4. Submerge and cook for 24 minutes
5. Take a large bowl and add tomato, avocado, jalapeno, cilantro
6. Toss well
7. Top the salad with the cooked contents from the bag
8. Toss and serve
9. Enjoy!

NUTRITION VALUES (PER SERVING)

- Calories: 148
- Fat: 2g
- Carbohydrates: 7g
- Protein: 24g

Scallops And Citrus Sauce

SERVING: 4

PREP TIME: 15 MINUTES

COOK TIME: 30 MINUTES

INGREDIENTS

- 2 pounds scallops, cleaned
- 2 lemons, quartered
- 2 tablespoons ghee
- 2 shallots, chopped
- ¼ cup pink grapefruit juice
- ¼ cup orange juice
- 2 tablespoons acacia honey
- Salt and pepper to taste

HOW TO

1. Prepare your water bath by submerging your Sous Vide immersion circulator and raise the temperature to 122 degree F
2. Rinse scallops and drain them
3. Season scallops with salt, pepper and divide between two large Sous Vide zip bags
4. Place 2 quarter lemons in each bag and seal using immersion method
5. Submerge and cook for 30 minutes
6. Take a saucepan and place it over heat, melt ghee
7. Add chopped shallots, cook for 4 minutes
8. Remove scallops from bag and sear both sides on greases skillet
9. Remove scallops from skillet
10. Deglaze pan with orange juice and pour grapefruit juice and lemon juice
11. Add shallots, lemon zest
12. Simmer until sauce reduces to half
13. Stir in honey, simmer until thick
14. Serve scallops with the sauce
15. Enjoy!

NUTRITION VALUES (PER SERVING)

- Calories: 279
- Fat: 8g
- Carbohydrates: 11g
- Protein: 38g

Salmon With Yogurt and Dill Sauce

SERVING: 2

PREP TIME: 10 HOURS

COOK TIME: 20 MINUTES

INGREDIENTS

- 2 salmon fillets
- ½ teaspoon salt
- ½ teaspoon pepper
- 2-4 sprigs, fresh dill

FOR SAUCE

- 1 cup Greek yogurt
- 1 tablespoon fresh dill, minced
- Juice of 1 lemon
- ½ teaspoon salt
- ½ teaspoon pepper

HOW TO

1. Prepare your water bath by submerging your Sous Vide immersion circulator and raise the temperature to 140 degree F
2. Season salmon and pepper and transfer to a zip bag
3. Add dill and seal using immersion method, let it refrigerate for ½ hour
4. Submerge the bag underwater and let it cook for 20 minutes
5. Prepare the sauce by mixing all the sauce ingredients in a bowl and season it well
6. Once salmon is cooked, serve with the sauce and enjoy!

NUTRITION VALUES (PER SERVING)

- Calories: 498
- Fat: 19g
- Carbohydrates: 10g
- Protein: 70g

Simple Clam Sauce And Linguine

SERVING: 3

PREP TIME: 20 MINUTES

COOK TIME: 20 MINUTES

INGREDIENTS

- 2 dozen clams, cleaned
- 2 tablespoons butter
- 1 tablespoon flour
- 3 garlic cloves, minced
- ¼ cup white wine
- 1 teaspoon pepper
- ¼ cup fresh basil, chopped
- Cooked linguine for serving

HOW TO

1. Prepare your water bath by submerging your Sous Vide immersion circulator and raise the temperature to 180 degree F
2. Transfer clams to your Sous Vide zip bag and seal using immersion method
3. Submerge and cook for 15 minutes
4. Take a pan and place it over medium heat
5. Add butter and melt
6. Add garlic and stir
7. Add flour and cook until bubbling subsides, pour wine
8. Keep stirring until sauce thickens
9. Once clams are ready, remove them from zip bag and transfer to the cooking liquid
10. Stir in basil
11. Serve clam sauce with cooked linguine
12. Enjoy!

NUTRITION VALUES (PER SERVING)

- Calories: 292
- Fat: 13g
- Carbohydrates: 12g
- Protein: 26g

Secret Swordfish Picatta Dish

SERVING: 3

PREP TIME: 20 MINUTES

COOK TIME: 30 MINUTES

INGREDIENTS

- 2 swordfish steak
- 1 teaspoon salt
- 1 teaspoon pepper
- 2 tablespoons olive oil
- ¼ cup butter
- 2 cloves garlic, minced
- 2 tablespoons lemon juice
- 2 tablespoons capers, with juice
- 2 tablespoons fresh basil, chopped

HOW TO

1. Prepare your water bath by submerging your Sous Vide immersion circulator and raise the temperature to 140 degree F
2. Season swordfish with salt and pepper
3. Transfer to zip bag and seal using immersion method
4. Cook for 30 minutes
5. Take a pan and melt butter and olive oil, add garlic and cook for 30 seconds
6. Stir in lemon juice, capers with juice and basil
7. Once the swordfish is done, transfer to plate and serve, topped with sauce
8. Enjoy!

NUTRITION VALUES (PER SERVING)

- Calories: 623
- Fat: 49g
- Carbohydrates: 3g
- Protein: 39g

Generous Shrimp Scamp

SERVING: 2

PREP TIME: 20 MINUTES

COOK TIME: 40 MINUTES

INGREDIENTS

- 1 pound shrimp, shelled
- ¼ cup butter
- 3 cloves garlic, minced
- ½ cup white wine
- ¼ cup fresh parsley, chopped
- Juice of half a lemon
- ½ teaspoon salt
- 1 teaspoon pepper
- Cooked pasta for serving

HOW TO

1. Prepare your water bath by submerging your Sous Vide immersion circulator and raise the temperature to 147 degree F
2. Transfer shrimp to Sous Vide zip bag and seal using immersion method
3. Submerge and cook for 30 minutes
4. Take pan and melt butter over medium heat
5. Add garlic and cook for 30 seconds
6. Add white wine and lemon juice, cook until reduced by half
7. Once shrimps are ready, add the shrimp to the pan alongside any cooking juice
8. Stir in parsley
9. Season with salt and pepper
10. Serve on top of cooked pasta
11. Enjoy!

NUTRITION VALUES (PER SERVING)

- Calories: 461
- Fat: 24g
- Carbohydrates: 5g
- Protein: 46g

Fancy Bacon And Sole Fish

SERVING: 3

PREP TIME: 10 MINUTES

COOK TIME: 25 MINUTES

INGREDIENTS

- 2 - 5 ounces each, sole fish fillets
- 2 tablespoons olive oil
- 2 slices bacon
- ½ tablespoon lemon juice
- Salt and pepper to taste

HOW TO

1. Prepare your water bath by submerging your Sous Vide immersion circulator and raise the temperature to 132 degree F
2. Take a non-stick skillet and place it over medium heat, add bacon and cook until crispy
3. Remove bacon and keep it on the side
4. Season fish fillets with salt, pepper and lemon juice
5. Brush fish with olive oil
6. Transfer fish to Sous Vide zip bag and top with bacon
7. Seal using immersion method
8. Submerge and cook for 25 minutes
9. Remove and serve
10. Enjoy!

NUTRITION VALUES (PER SERVING)

- Calories: 298
- Fat: 22g
- Carbohydrates: 0.4g
- Protein: 22g

Wholesome Red Snapper

SERVING: 2

PREP TIME: 20 MINUTES

COOK TIME: 1 HOUR

INGREDIENTS

- 1 small red snapper, cleaned and gutted
- 1 teaspoon salt
- 1 teaspoon pepper
- 4 garlic cloves, crushed
- 2 sprigs rosemary
- 1 lemon, cut into wedges
- 2 tablespoons butter, cut into parts

HOW TO

1. Prepare your water bath by submerging your Sous Vide immersion circulator and raise the temperature to 140 degree F
2. Season fish with salt and pepper
3. Stuff center of fish with garlic, rosemary, half of lemon and butter
4. Seal using immersion method and cook for 60 minutes underwater
5. Serve fish with lemon wedges

NUTRITION VALUES (PER SERVING)

- Calories: 800
- Fat: 20g
- Carbohydrates: 4g
- Protein: 140g

Juicy Coriander And Garlic Squid Delight

SERVING: 4

PREP TIME: 20 MINUTES

COOK TIME: 2 HOURS

INGREDIENTS

- 4 pieces 4 ounces squids, cleaned
- ¼ cup olive oil
- ¼ cup coriander, chopped
- 4 garlic cloves, minced
- 2 chili pepper, chopped
- 2 teaspoons ginger, minced
- ¼ cup vegetable oil
- 1 lemon ,cut into wedges
- Salt and pepper to taste

HOW TO

1. Prepare your water bath by submerging your Sous Vide immersion circulator and raise the temperature to 136 degree F
2. Add squids, 2 tablespoons olive oil to Sous Vide zip bags
3. Season and seal using immersion method
4. Submerge and cook for 2 hours
5. Take a skillet and place it over medium heat
6. Add olive oil and let it heat up
7. Add garlic chili pepper, ginger and cook for 1 minute
8. Add half of coriander and stir
9. Remove heat
10. Remove cooked squids from bag
11. Heat up more oil in skillet and wait until sizzling hot, add squid and cook for 30 seconds per side
12. Transfer squids onto plate and top with garlic-coriander mix
13. Sprinkle remaining coriander
14. Serve with lemon
15. Enjoy!

NUTRITION VALUES (PER SERVING)

- Calories: 346
- Fat: 27g
- Carbohydrates: 6g
- Protein: 18g

Chapter 8: Beef Recipes

Juicy Spiced Ribs

SERVING: 4

PREP TIME: 10 MINUTES

COOK TIME: 24 MINUTES

INGREDIENTS

- 1 and ½ pounds baby back ribs
- 1 tablespoon fine salt
- 1 tablespoon brown sugar
- 1 tablespoon smoked paprika
- ½ tablespoon ground cumin
- ½ tablespoon ground coriander
- ½ tablespoon pepper
- ¼ tablespoon dried garlic
- 1 tablespoon dried parsley
- ½ cup BBQ Sauce

HOW TO

1. Prepare your water bath by submerging your Sous Vide immersion circulator and raise the temperature to 155 degree F
2. Take a bowl and add the listed spices and parsley, mix well
3. Rub the ribs with the prepared spice mix
4. Transfer ribs to a Sous Vide zip bag and seal using immersion method
5. Submerge underwater and cook for 24 hours
6. Once done, remove the bag from water bath
7. Pre-heat your grill and grill ribs for 7-8 minutes, making sure to keep basting it with BBQ sauce
8. Serve and enjoy!

NUTRITION VALUES (PER SERVING)

- Calories: 446
- Fat: 21g
- Carbohydrates: 15g
- Protein: 45g

Authentic BBQ Beef Brisket

SERVING: 8

PREP TIME: 20 MINUTES

COOK TIME: 48 HOURS 20 MINUTES

INGREDIENTS

- 1 whole 5 pounds beef brisket
- ¼ cup coarsely ground pepper
- ¼ cup coarsely ground salt
- 1 tablespoon olive oil
- Split rolls for serving
- Sliced pickles for serving

HOW TO

1. Prepare your water bath by submerging your Sous Vide immersion circulator and raise the temperature to 150 degree F
2. Rub salt and pepper over the brisket
3. Transfer to zip bag and seal using immersion method
4. Cook for 48 hours
5. Remove brisket from bag
6. Sear both sides with oil in a hot pan
7. Slice thinly across the grain and serve on rolls with pickles
8. Enjoy!

NUTRITION VALUES (PER SERVING)

- Calories: 576
- Fat: 43g
- Carbohydrates: 0.4g
- Protein: 41g

Exquisite Beef Tri-Tip

SERVING: 6

PREP TIME: 20 MINUTES

COOK TIME: 6 HOURS

INGREDIENTS

- 2 and ½ pounds beef tri-tip
- 2 teaspoons salt
- 1 teaspoon fresh ground black pepper
- ½ cup BBQ sauce
- 2 teaspoons light brown sugar

HOW TO

1. Prepare your water bath by submerging your Sous Vide immersion circulator and raise the temperature to 130 degree F
2. Season beef with 1 teaspoon salt and ½ teaspoon pepper
3. Transfer to a Sous Vide zip bag , add ¼ cup BBQ sauce and seal using immersion method
4. Submerge and let it cook for 6 hours
5. Once the timer goes off, remove bag from water
6. Pat the meat dry
7. Pre-heat your broiler to medium and transfer meat to a foil-lined baking sheet
8. Brush meat with remaining BBQ sauce and sprinkle sugar, salt and pepper
9. Broil for 5 minutes until caramelized
10. Let it rest for 5 minutes, slice and serve
11. Enjoy!

NUTRITION VALUES (PER SERVING)

- Calories: 163
- Fat: 5g
- Carbohydrates: 8g
- Protein: 18g

Juicy Corned Beef

SERVING: 6

PREP TIME: 5 MINUTES

COOK TIME: 48 HOURS

INGREDIENTS

- 2-2½ lbs. corned beef, uncooked and pre-brined
- 1 whole Cabbage

HOW TO

1. Prepare your water bath by submerging your Sous Vide immersion circulator and raise the temperature to 140 degree F
2. Unwrap your pre-brined corned beef and pat dry using kitchen towel
3. Place the corned beef in a resealable bag
4. Seal using the immersion method, submerge and cook for 48 hours
5. When done, chop the cabbage into quarters and remove the core
6. Slice into ½ inch strips
7. Remove the meat from the bath
8. Place a pan over medium heat
9. Add the juice from the bag and allow to boil
10. Add the chopped cabbage and cook until the liquid has evaporated
11. Transfer the cooked cabbage to your serving plate
12. Serve by placing the beef on the cabbage

NUTRITION VALUES (PER SERVING)

- Calories: 522
- Fat: 27g
- Carbohydrates: 48g
- Protein: 22g

The Easy Beef Wellington

SERVING: 4

PREP TIME: 60 MINUTES

COOK TIME: 2 HOURS

INGREDIENTS

- 1 lb. beef tenderloin fillet
- Salt and pepper as needed
- 2 tablespoons Dijon mustard
- 1 sheet puff pastry, thawed
- 8 oz. cremini mushrooms
- 1 shallot, diced
- 3 cloves garlic, chopped
- 1 tablespoon unsalted butter
- 6 slices prosciutto

HOW TO

1. Prepare your water bath by submerging your Sous Vide immersion circulator and raise the temperature to 124 degree F
2. Season the beef tenderloin with salt and pepper
3. Place in a zip bag and seal using the immersion method. Cook for 2 hours
4. Chop the mushrooms in a food processor
5. Put the shallots and garlic in a hot pan
6. Cook until tender, add the chopped mushrooms and cook until water has evaporated
7. Add 1 tablespoon of butter and cook
8. Remove the beef and pat dry
9. Heat the oil in a cast iron pan until shimmering. Sear the beef on all sides for 30 seconds
10. Spread the Dijon mustard all over the tenderloin
11. Lay a plastic wrap on a surface and arrange your prosciutto slices horizontally. Spread the duxelles* thinly over the prosciutto and place the tenderloin on top
12. Roll the tender loin in the plastic wrap tightly and chill for 20 minutes

13. Roll out your thawed pastry and brush with egg wash. Unwrap the tender loin and place in the pastry puff
14. Bake for 10 minutes in your oven at 475-degrees Fahrenheit
15. Slice and serve!

NUTRITION VALUES (PER SERVING)

- Calories: 354
- Fat: 22g
- Carbohydrates: 11g
- Protein: 25g

Mazing Prime Rib

SERVING: 12

PREP TIME: 45 MINUTES

COOK TIME: 6 HOURS

INGREDIENTS

- 3 lbs. bone-in beef Ribeye roast
- Kosher salt
- 1 tablespoon black peppercorn, coarsely ground
- 1 tablespoon green peppercorn, coarsely ground
- 1 tablespoon pink peppercorn, coarsely ground
- 1 tablespoon dried celery seeds
- 2 tablespoons dried garlic powder
- 4 sprigs rosemary
- 1-quart beef stock
- 2 egg whites

HOW TO

1. Season the beef with kosher salt and chill for 12 hours
2. Prepare your water bath by submerging your Sous Vide immersion circulator and raise the temperature to 132 degree F
3. Put the beef in a zip bag and seal using the immersion method
4. Cook for 6 hours
5. Preheat the oven to 425-degrees Fahrenheit and remove the beef. Pat it dry
6. Whisk the peppercorns, celery seeds, garlic powder and rosemary together in a bowl
7. Brush the top of your cooked roast with egg white and season with the mixture and salt
8. Place the roast on a baking rack and roast for 10-15 minutes. Allow it to rest for 10-15 minutes and carve
9. Put the cooking liquid from the bag in a large saucepan, bring to a boil and simmer until the amount has halved.
10. Carve the roast and serve with the juice

NUTRITION VALUES (PER SERVING)

- Calories: 354
- Fat: 22g
- Carbohydrates: 11g
- Protein: 25g

Grandermother's Beef Brisket

SERVING: 12

PREP TIME: 45 MINUTES

COOK TIME: 6 HOURS

INGREDIENTS

- 6 pounds beef brisket
- 2 tablespoons extra virgin-olive oil
- 4 large shallots, peeled and thinly sliced
- 4 garlic cloves, peeled and smashed
- ¼ cup apple cider vinegar
- ½ cup apple cider
- ½ cup ketchup
- ½ cup honey
- ¼ cup Dijon mustard
- 2 cups Dr. Pepper
- 1 tablespoon whole black peppercorns
- 2 dried bay leaves
- 2 dried allspice berries
- 2 dried whole cloves
- Kosher salt to taste

HOW TO

1. Prepare your water bath by submerging your Sous Vide immersion circulator and raise the temperature to 155 degree F
2. Place a large sized iron skillet over high heat, add the olive oil and heat until it starts smoking
3. Add the brisket and sear until golden brown on both sides
4. Remove the brisket and keep it on the side. Put the shallots and garlic in the pan and reduce the heat to medium
5. Sauté for 10 minutes
6. Take a bowl and whisk in the vinegar, apple cider, honey, ketchup, mustard, peppercorn, bay leaves, Dr. Pepper, allspice and cloves. Add the mixture to the shallots and remove from the heat

7. Place the brisket and sauce in a zip bag and seal using the immersion method. Cook for 48 hours
8. Remove from the bag and dry. Broil for 5 minutes
9. Put the cooking liquid in a saucepan and simmer for 10 minutes over medium high heat
10. Serve with the brisket

NUTRITION VALUES (PER SERVING)

- Calories: 588
- Fat: 22g
- Carbohydrates: 22g
- Protein: 21g

Chapter 9: Potato Recipes

Amazing Potato Confit

SERVING: 4

PREP TIME: 15 MINUTES

COOK TIME: 1 HOUR

INGREDIENTS

- 1 pound small red potatoes
- 1 teaspoon kosher salt
- ¼ teaspoon ground black pepper
- 2 tablespoons whole butter
- 1 tablespoon corn oil

HOW TO

1. Prepare your water bath by submerging your Sous Vide immersion circulator and raise the temperature to 190 degree F
2. Cut potatoes in half and season with rosemary, salt and pepper
3. Take a bowl and mix in potatoes, oil and butter
4. Transfer to heavy-duty Sous Vide zip bag and seal using immersion method
5. Submerge and cook for 60 minutes
6. Transfer to bowl and add extra butter
7. Enjoy!

NUTRITION VALUES (PER SERVING)

- Calories: 314
- Fat: 10g
- Carbohydrates: 53g
- Protein: 8g

Garlic And Rosemary Potato Mash

SERVING: 4

PREP TIME: 25 MINUTES

COOK TIME: 1 HOUR 30 MINUTES

INGREDIENTS

- 2 pounds russet potatoes
- 5 garlic cloves
- 8 ounces unsalted butter
- 1 cup whole milk
- 3 sprigs rosemary
- Salt and pepper as needed

HOW TO

1. Prepare your water bath by submerging your Sous Vide immersion circulator and raise the temperature to 194 degree F
2. Rinse potatoes thoroughly under cold water and peel
3. Slice them into 1/8 inch thick rounds
4. Peel garlic cloves and mash
5. Add potatoes, garlic, butter, 2 teaspoon salt and rosemary into a heavy duty Sous Vide zip bag
6. Seal using immersion method
7. Submerge and cook for 1 and ½ hours
8. Strain mix and pour into medium bowl
9. Transfer potatoes to large sized bowl and mash using potato masher
10. Stir in melted butter, milk into mashed potato
11. Season with salt and pepper and garnish with rosemary
12. Serve and enjoy!

NUTRITION VALUES (PER SERVING)

- Calories: 185
- Fat: 6g
- Carbohydrates: 6g
- Protein: 6g

Potato Salad

SERVING: 6

PREP TIME: 10 MINUTES

COOK TIME: 1 HOUR AND 30 MINUTES

INGREDIENTS

- 1 and ½ pounds yellow potatoes or red potatoes
- 4 ounce thick cut bacon, sliced into about ¼-inch slices
- ½ cup chicken stock
- 1/3 cup cider vinegar
- 4 scallions, thinly sliced
- ½ cup onion, chopped
- Salt and pepper, to taste

HOW TO

1. Prepare your water bath by submerging your Sous Vide immersion circulator and raise the temperature to 185 degree F
2. Cut potatoes into ¾-inch thick cubes
3. Place chicken stock and potatoes to a Sous Vide zip bags and seal using immersion method
4. Submerge underwater and cook for 1 hour and 30 minutes
5. Meanwhile, take a non-stick skillet over medium-high heat just 15 minutes before Sous Vide cook ends
6. Add bacon and cook until crisp
7. Remove bacon and add chopped onions
8. Cook for 5 to 7 minutes or soften
9. Add vinegar and cook until reduced slightly
10. Once done, remove potatoes from water bath
11. Place them in skillet, with the cooking water
12. Until liquid thickens continue cooking for few more minutes
13. Remove potatoes from the heat
14. Stir in scallions and toss to combine
15. Serve while still hot and enjoy!

NUTRITION VALUES (PER SERVING)

- Calories: 108
- Fat: 1.6g
- Carbohydrates: 19.9g
- Protein: 3.7g

Creamy Potato Mash

SERVING: 6

PREP TIME: 5 MINUTES

COOK TIME: 1 HOUR

INGREDIENTS

- 1 pound russet potatoes, peeled and sliced
- 8 tablespoons butter
- ½ cup heavy cream
- 1 teaspoon salt

HOW TO

1. Prepare your water bath by submerging your Sous Vide immersion circulator and raise the temperature to 190 degree F
2. Put the heavy cream, russet potatoes, kosher salt, and butter into a heavy-duty zip bag and seal using the immersion method*
3. Submerge and cook for 60 minutes
4. Pass the contents through a food processor into a large bowl
5. Mix well and serve!

NUTRITION VALUES (PER SERVING)

- Calories: 206
- Fat: 7g
- Carbohydrates: 34g
- Protein: 5g

Mini Fingerling Potatoes

SERVING: 4

PREP TIME: 10 MINUTES

COOK TIME: 45 MINUTES

INGREDIENTS

- 8 ounces fingerling potatoes
- Salt, to taste
- Pepper, to taste
- 1 tablespoon unsalted vegan butter
- 1 sprig rosemary

HOW TO

1. Prepare your water bath by submerging your Sous Vide immersion circulator and raise the temperature to 178 degree F
2. Season the potatoes with salt and pepper and transfer them to resealable bag.
3. Seal using the immersion method and submerge the bag under water and cook for 45 minutes.
4. Once done, remove the bag and potatoes.
5. Cut the potatoes in half (lengthwise).
6. Take a large skillet and place it over medium-high heat.
7. Add the butter and allow it to melt, add rosemary and the potatoes.
8. Cook for 3 minutes and transfer to a plate.
9. Serve by seasoning it with a bit of salt if needed

NUTRITION VALUES (PER SERVING)

- Calories: 141
- Fat: 6g
- Carbohydrates: 19g
- Protein: 5g

Sweet Potatoes And Pecans

SERVING: 2

PREP TIME: 45 MINUTES

COOK TIME: 3 HOURS

INGREDIENTS

- 1 pound sweet potatoes sliced up into ¼ inch thick rounds
- ½ teaspoon kosher salt
- ¼ cup pecans
- 1 tablespoon coconut oil

HOW TO

1. Prepare your water bath by submerging your Sous Vide immersion circulator and raise the temperature to 145 degree F
2. Add the potatoes and salt to your resealable bag and seal using the immersion method
3. Transfer the bag to the water bath and cook for 3 hours.
4. Toast the pecans in a dry skillet over medium heat.
5. Transfer the pecans to a cutting board and chop them up.
6. Pre-heat your oven to 375-degrees Fahrenheit and line a rimmed baking sheet with parchment paper.
7. Transfer the potatoes to a bowl and toss with coconut oil.
8. Spread the potatoes on the baking sheet and bake for 20-30 minutes, making sure to flip once.
9. Transfer to serving platter and serve with a sprinkle of toasted pecans.

NUTRITION VALUES (PER SERVING)

- Calories: 195
- Fat: 6g
- Carbohydrates: 30g
- Protein: 6g

Delicious Candied Potatoes

SERVING: 6

PREP TIME: 45 MINUTES

COOK TIME: 2 HOURS

INGREDIENTS

- 2 pounds' sweet potatoes, peeled up and cut into ¼ slices
- ½ cup unsalted butter
- ¼ cup maple syrup
- 2 oranges, juice and zest
- 1 teaspoon kosher salt
- 1 cup chopped walnuts
- 1 cinnamon stick
- ¼ cup brown sugar

HOW TO

1. Prepare your water bath by submerging your Sous Vide immersion circulator and raise the temperature to 155 degree F
2. Take a resealable bag and add the sweet potatoes and ¼ cup of butter.
3. Seal using the immersion method and cook for 2 hours.
4. Pre-heat your oven to 350-degrees Fahrenheit.
5. Remove the potatoes from the bag and pat dry.
6. Arrange the potatoes evenly in a baking dish.
7. Take a medium saucepan and bring ¼ cup of butter, brown sugar, maple syrup, orange zest and juice, walnuts, salt, and cinnamon stick to a boil.
8. Remove from heat and pour over sweet potatoes, discard the cinnamon stick
9. Bake for 30 minutes and serve warm!

NUTRITION VALUES (PER SERVING)

- Calories: 320
- Fat: 5g
- Carbohydrates: 67g
- Protein: 3g

Chapter 10: Fruits and Vegetables Recipes

Tasty Hazelnut Green Beans

SERVING: 8

PREP TIME: 5 MINUTES

COOK TIME: 1 HOUR

INGREDIENTS

- 2 pounds green beans, trimmed
- 2 mandarins
- 2 tablespoons butter
- ½ teaspoon salt
- 2 ounces hazelnuts

HOW TO

1. Prepare your water bath by submerging your Sous Vide immersion circulator and raise the temperature to 185 degree F
2. Add green beans, salt, butter to a large heavy duty Sous Vide zip bag
3. Add mandarin zest and squeeze mandarin juice
4. Keep extra juice for later use
5. Seal using immersion method
6. Submerge and cook for 1 hour
7. Remove beans from bath and transfer to serving paltter, add extra zest and juice
8. Garnish with hazelnuts
9. Enjoy!

NUTRITION VALUES (PER SERVING)

- Calories: 136
- Fat: 12g
- Carbohydrates: 8g
- Protein: 2g

Hearty Pear And Walnut Salad

SERVING: 4

PREP TIME: 10 MINUTES

COOK TIME: 30 MINUTES

INGREDIENTS

- 2 tablespoons honey
- 2 pears, cored, halved and thinly sliced
- ½ cup walnuts, lightly toasted, roughly chopped
- ½ cup parmesan, shaved
- 4 cups arugula
- Salt as needed

GARLIC DIJON DRESSING

- ¼ cup olive oil
- 1 tablespoon white wine vinegar
- 1 teaspoon Dijon mustard
- 1 garlic clove, minced
- Salt as needed

HOW TO

1. Prepare your water bath by submerging your Sous Vide immersion circulator and raise the temperature to 159 degree F
2. Take a micro-wave proof bowl and add honey, heat for 20 seconds
3. Add pears in honey and mix well
4. Transfer to heavy-duty re-sealable zip bag and seal using immersion method
5. Submerge and cook for 30 minutes, transfer to ice-water bath and let it cool for 5 minutes
6. Chill for 3 hours
7. Take a bowl and add dressing ingredients, shake well
8. Let it cool as well
9. Serve by transferring walnuts, arugula, parmesan to a large bowl and adding drained slices of pear and dressing

10. Toss and season accordingly
11. Serve and enjoy!

NUTRITION VALUES (PER SERVING)

- Calories: 377
- Fat: 14g
- Carbohydrates: 56g
- Protein: 5g

Juicy Shallot And Cream Peas

SERVING: 6

PREP TIME: 5 MINUTES

COOK TIME: 1 HOUR

INGREDIENTS

- 1 pound frozen sweet peas
- 1 cu heavy cream
- ¼ cup butter
- 1 tablespoon cornstarch
- ¼ teaspoon ground nutmeg
- 4 cloves
- 2 bay leaves
- Fresh ground black pepper

HOW TO

1. Prepare your water bath by submerging your Sous Vide immersion circulator and raise the temperature to 183 degree F
2. Add cream, nutmeg, cornstarch in a small bowl and mix well until cornstarch dissolves
3. Add listed ingredients to a Sous Vide zip bag and seal using immersion method
4. Submerge and cook for 1 hour
5. Remove and garnish with pepper
6. Serve and enjoy!

NUTRITION VALUES (PER SERVING)

- Calories: 519
- Fat: 46g
- Carbohydrates: 14g
- Protein: 6g

Exquisite Sous Vide Cactus

SERVING: 4

PREP TIME: 15 MINUTES

COOK TIME: 1 HOUR

INGREDIENTS

- 2 tablespoons freshly squeezed lime juice
- 1 tablespoon canola oil
- 1 clove garlic, thinly sliced
- 1 teaspoon ground coriander
- 1 teaspoon ground cumin
- 1 teaspoon salt
- 4 cactus paddles, thorns removed

HOW TO

1. Prepare your water bath by submerging your Sous Vide immersion circulator and raise the temperature to 175 degree F
2. Take a bowl and whisk in lime juice, garlic, oil, coriander, cumin, salt and mix well
3. Transfer the whole mixture alongside cactus to a Sous Vide zip bag and seal using immersion method
4. Submerge and cook for 60 minutes
5. Remove and drain cactus, discard cooking liquid
6. Use a veggie peeler to remove skin from cactus into strips
7. Serve and enjoy!

NUTRITION VALUES (PER SERVING)

- Calories: 59
- Fat: 2g
- Carbohydrates: 11g
- Protein: 2g

Momofuku Clear Brussels

SERVING: 4

PREP TIME: 20 MINUTES

COOK TIME: 50 MINUTES

INGREDIENTS

- 2 pounds Brussels, stems trimmed and sliced in half
- 2 tablespoons extra-virgin olive oil
- ¼ teaspoon salt
- ¼ cup fish sauce
- 2 tablespoons water
- 1 and ½ tablespoons granulated sugar
- 1 tablespoon rice vinegar
- 1 and ½ teaspoons lime juice
- 12 thinly sliced Thai chilies
- 1 small garlic clove, minced
- Chopped fresh mint for serving
- Chopped fresh cilantro for serving

HOW TO

1. Prepare your water bath by submerging your Sous Vide immersion circulator and raise the temperature to 183 degree F
2. Add Brussels sprouts, olive oil, salt to heavy duty zip bag and seal using immersion method
3. Submerge and cook for 50 minutes
4. Add fish sauce, sugar, water, rice vinegar, lime juice, garlic, chilis to a small sized bowl and mix well to prepare the vinaigrette
5. Take an aluminum lined baking sheet and add Brussels
6. Set up your broiler and broil Brussels for 5 minutes until charred
7. Transfer to a medium bowl and add vinaigrette, mix and toss with mint and cilantro
8. Serve and enjoy!

NUTRITION VALUES (PER SERVING)

- Calories: 610
- Fat: 5g
- Carbohydrates: 38g
- Protein: 10g

Sensational Onion Julienne

SERVING: 10

PREP TIME: 3 HOURS 10 MINUTES

COOK TIME: 2 HOURS

INGREDIENTS

- 2 brown onions, julienned
- 2 tablespoons olive oil
- 1 tablespoon balsamic vinegar
- 2 tablespoon brown sugar
- Salt and pepper to taste

HOW TO

1. Prepare your water bath by submerging your Sous Vide immersion circulator and raise the temperature to 185 degree F
2. Add listed ingredients to a Sous Vide heavy duty zip bag
3. Seal using immersion method
4. Submerge and let it cook for 2 hours
5. Transfer the container to your fridge and chill for 3 hours
6. Serve and enjoy!

NUTRITION VALUES (PER SERVING)

- Calories: 176
- Fat: 3g
- Carbohydrates: 24g
- Protein: 3g

Delicious Butter Radish

SERVING: 4

PREP TIME: 15 MINUTES

COOK TIME: 45 MINUTES

INGREDIENTS

- 1 pound radish, halved
- 3 tablespoons unsalted butter
- 1 teaspoon salt
- ½ teaspoon freshly ground black pepper

HOW TO

1. Prepare your water bath by submerging your Sous Vide immersion circulator and raise the temperature to 180 degree F
2. Add listed ingredients to a heavy duty zip bag and seal using immersion method
3. Submerge and cook for 45 minutes
4. Once done, remove bag and transfer contents to platter
5. Serve and enjoy!

NUTRITION VALUES (PER SERVING)

- Calories: 248
- Fat: 1g
- Carbohydrates: 31g
- Protein: 1g

Thyme Lard Broad Beans

SERVING: 4

PREP TIME: 10 MINUTES

COOK TIME: 1 HOUR

INGREDIENTS

- 1 and ½ pounds broad beans
- 3 ounce lard
- 4 springs thyme
- 1 pinch red pepper flakes

HOW TO

1. Prepare your water bath by submerging your Sous Vide immersion circulator and raise the temperature to 176 degree F
2. Trim the beans and blanch in simmering water for 30 seconds
3. Rinse the beans under cold water
4. Between two bags divide the beans and add two springs thyme per bag
5. Chop the lard and sprinkle over the beans, along with red pepper flakes
6. Transfer the bag to a Sous Vide zip bags and seal using immersion method
7. Submerge underwater and cook for 1 hour
8. Once done, remove the beans from water bath
9. Submerge it in ice-cold water for 2-3 minutes
10. Serve the beans and enjoy!

NUTRITION VALUES (PER SERVING)

- Calories: 265
- Fat: 21.6g
- Carbohydrates: 13.9g
- Protein: 4.1g

Sous Vide Vegetable and Fruit Recipes

SERVING: 4

PREP TIME: 20 MINUTES

COOK TIME: 30 MINUTES

INGREDIENTS

- 20 spears white asparagus, trimmed
- 1 tablespoon salt
- 2 orange slices
- 2 tablespoons butter
- ½ cup orange juice
- 2 eggs
- ¼ cup butter
- ½ tablespoon lemon juice
- Salt and pepper, to taste

HOW TO

1. Prepare your water bath by submerging your Sous Vide immersion circulator and raise the temperature to 185 degree F
2. Transfer asparagus, orange juice, butter, orange slices and salt to a Sous Vide zip bag and seal using immersion method
3. Submerge underwater and cook for 25 minutes
4. Take a large skillet and heat over medium-high heat
5. Take out asparagus from the zip bag and transfer to the skillet
6. Cook for 30 seconds and remove
7. To make the sauce; take a heat-proof bowl and add the yolks and set the bowl over simmering water
8. Melt butter over medium heat
9. Add butter to eggs yolk, whisking rapidly
10. Continue until all butter mixed well
11. Stir in the lemon juice, season it to taste
12. Top with sauce and serve asparagus

NUTRITION VALUES (PER SERVING)

- Calories: 109
- Fat: 10.01g
- Carbohydrates: 5.6g
- Protein: 4.8g

Chapter 11: Dessert Recipes

Sassy Peach Cobbler

SERVING: 6

PREP TIME: 20 MINUTES

COOK TIME: 3 HOURS

INGREDIENTS

- 3 cups freestone, peaches, peeled and diced
- 8 tablespoons unsalted butter
- 1 cup granulated sugar
- 1 teaspoon vanilla extract
- 1 teaspoon almond extract
- 1 cup whole milk
- 1 cup self-rising flour

HOW TO

1. Prepare your water bath by submerging your Sous Vide immersion circulator and raise the temperature to 195 degree F
2. Take a 235 ml canning jar and grease it up well
3. Divide freestone peaches evenly between the jars
4. Add sugar, butter to a medium sized bowl and blend for 5 minutes on medium
5. Lower heat and add almond extract, whole milk, vanilla extract and mix well
6. Add self-rising flour and mix until no lumps
7. Pour batter into canning jar and gently tighten the lid
8. Submerge and cook for 3 hours
9. Open lid and brown the top with blowtorch
10. Serve and enjoy!

NUTRITION VALUES (PER SERVING)

- Calories: 524
- Fat: 19g
- Carbohydrates: 62g
- Protein: 6g

Curried Acorn Squash

SERVING: 4

PREP TIME: 30 MINUTES

COOK TIME: 2 HOURS

INGREDIENTS

- 1 acorn squash, seeded and cut into wedges
- 1 tablespoon curry powder or garam masala
- ¼ teaspoon salt
- 2 tablespoons butter

HOW TO

1. Prepare your water bath by submerging your Sous Vide immersion circulator and raise the temperature to 185 degree
2. Transfer all ingredients to a Sous Vide zip bag and seal using immersion method
3. Cook for 1 and ½ hours to 2 hours
4. Once done, remove the bag from water bath
5. Serve and enjoy!

NUTRITION VALUES (PER SERVING)

- Calories: 99
- Fat: 6.09g
- Carbohydrates: 12.11g
- Protein: 1.15g

Smoked Salmon Eggs Benedict

SERVING: 4

PREP TIME: 30 MINUTES

COOK TIME: 2 HOURS

INGREDIENTS

- 4 eggs
- 2 English muffins, split
- 8 ounces salmon, smoked
- Sous Vide Hollandaise sauce, bagged and uncooked

HOW TO

1. Prepare your water bath by submerging your Sous Vide immersion circulator and raise the temperature to 147 degree F
2. Place the bag of eggs and bag of hollandaise to a Sous Vide zip bags and seal using immersion method
3. Submerge underwater and cook for 2 hours
4. Toast and butter the English muffin before 30 minutes the end of cooking time
5. Once done, remove the bags from water bath
6. Pour sauce into a blender and blend properly
7. Meanwhile, take a bowl of cold water and let eggs cold
8. Arrange 2 ounces of smoked salmon on each English muffin half to form a cup that will hold the poached egg
9. Crack each eggs over a slotted spoon held over a bowl
10. Allow the excess white to drip away
11. Keep one egg in each smoked cup
12. Drizzle with hollandaise sauce on top
13. Serve and enjoy!

NUTRITION VALUES (PER SERVING)

- Calories: 604
- Fat: 49g
- Carbohydrates: 15g
- Protein: 26.15g

Salty Custard

SERVING: 4

PREP TIME: 10 MINUTES

COOK TIME: 30 MINUTES

INGREDIENTS

- 8 large eggs
- 2 tablespoons sesame oil
- 2 cup chicken stock
- Salt and pepper, to taste
- Soy sauce, to garnish
- Green onion, chopped, to garnish

HOW TO

1. Prepare your water bath by submerging your Sous Vide immersion circulator and raise the temperature to 180 degree F
2. Add the listed ingredients excepts soy sauce and onion into your blender and blend until smooth
3. Strain through a fine-mesh sieve to remove any foam
4. Strain again and transfer into the vacuum bag, if needed
5. Transfer bag to a Sous Vide zip bag and seal using immersion method
6. Submerge underwater and cook for 20 minutes
7. Remove the bag from water bath and shake properly
8. Cook for additional 10 minutes
9. Once done, remove the bag from water bath
10. Place into ice cold bath for 20 minutes
11. Garnish them with splash of soy sauce and chopped green onion
12. Serve and enjoy!

NUTRITION VALUES (PER SERVING)

- Calories: 168
- Fat: 12.5g
- Carbohydrates: 1.1g
- Protein: 12.9g

Pears In Pomegranate Juice

SERVING: 8

PREP TIME: 20 MINUTES

COOK TIME: 30 MINUTES

INGREDIENTS

- 8 pears
- 5 cups pomegranate juice
- 1 cinnamon stick
- ¼ teaspoon allspice
- ¼ teaspoon nutmeg
- ¾ cup sugar
- ¼ teaspoon ground clove

HOW TO

1. Prepare your water bath by submerging your Sous Vide immersion circulator and raise the temperature to 176 degree F
2. Except the pears, combine all ingredients
3. Until the liquid is reduced by half, simmer it
4. Strain and place it aside
5. Peel if desired or scrub the pears
6. Transfer each pear in bag to a Sous Vide zip bags and seal using immersion method
7. Submerge underwater and cook for 30 minutes
8. Once done, remove the beans from water bath
9. Take a plate and remove pears carefully and slice them
10. Cook the juices in a saucepan until thick
11. Top them with pears
12. Serve the beans and enjoy!

NUTRITION VALUES (PER SERVING)

- Calories: 268
- Fat: 0.3g
- Carbohydrates: 59.4g
- Protein: 0.8g

Blueberry Lime Compote

SERVING: 4

PREP TIME: 10 MINUTES

COOK TIME: 1 HOUR

INGREDIENTS

- 1 pound blueberries, fresh
- ½ cup caster sugar
- 1 tablespoon lime juice
- 1 tablespoon lime zest
- 1 tablespoon tapioca starch

HOW TO

1. Prepare your water bath by submerging your Sous Vide immersion circulator and raise the temperature to 180 degree F
2. Take a large bowl, whisk the sugar, lime juice, lime zest and tapioca starch
3. Toss in blueberries and stir gently to coat
4. Transfer blueberries to a Sous Vide zip bags and seal using immersion method
5. Submerge underwater and cook for 1hour
6. Once done, remove the beans from water bath
7. Serve blueberries while hot and enjoy!

NUTRITION VALUES (PER SERVING)

- Calories: 171
- Fat: 0.4g
- Carbohydrates: 44.7g
- Protein: 0.9g

Tropical Pineapple

SERVING: 4

PREP TIME: 20 MINUTES

COOK TIME: 2 HOURS

INGREDIENTS

- 14 ounces pineapple, slices
- 1 cup brown sugar
- 1 vanilla pod, split, seeds, scraper
- ¼ cup rum

HOW TO

1. Prepare your water bath by submerging your Sous Vide immersion circulator and raise the temperature to 135 degree F
2. Transfer all ingredients to a Sous Vide zip bags and seal using immersion method
3. Submerge underwater and cook for 2hours
4. Once done, remove the beans from water bath
5. Take a saucepan, strain the pineapple liquid and keep the pineapple aside
6. Simmer the cooking juice until thickened
7. Now, take a bowl and drizzle with thickened sauce
8. Serve and enjoy!

NUTRITION VALUES (PER SERVING)

- Calories: 283
- Fat: 0.1g
- Carbohydrates: 48.7g
- Protein: 0.6g

Orange Compote

SERVING: 4

PREP TIME: 10 MINUTES

COOK TIME: 3 HOURS

INGREDIENTS

- 4 blood orange, quartered and thinly sliced
- 1 lemon, juice and zest
- ½ vanilla seed pod
- 1 teaspoon beef gelatin powder or agar agar
- 2 cups granulated sugar

HOW TO

1. Prepare your water bath by submerging your Sous Vide immersion circulator and raise the temperature to 190 degree F
2. Transfer all ingredients to a Sous Vide zip bags and seal using immersion method
3. Submerge underwater and cook for 3 hours
4. Once done, remove the beans from water bath
5. Place into an ice-cold water bath
6. Once cooled transfer into a food processor
7. Add the gelatin and process until smooth
8. Let it cool completely before serving
9. Serve and enjoy!

NUTRITION VALUES (PER SERVING)

- Calories: 466
- Fat: 0.3g
- Carbohydrates: 123.1g
- Protein: 1.6g

Pumpkin Crème Bruele

SERVING: 6

PREP TIME: 10 MINUTES

COOK TIME: 1 HOUR

INGREDIENTS

- 1 cup milk
- 1 cup heavy whipping cream
- 3 whole eggs
- 3 egg yolks
- ½ cup pumpkin puree
- ¼ cup maple syrup
- ½ teaspoon pumpkin spice
- A pinch of salt
- Granulated sugar

HOW TO

1. Prepare your water bath by submerging your Sous Vide immersion circulator and raise the temperature to 167 degree F
2. Take a large bowl and add the milk, heavy cream, 3 whole eggs, 3 egg yolks, ½ cup of pumpkin puree, ¼ cup of maple syrup, ½ teaspoon of pumpkin spice and a pinch of kosher salt.
3. Mix well and keep whisking until it is combined and smooth.
4. Pour the mixture into 6.4-ounce mason jars.
5. Place the lid loosely and cook for 1 hour
6. Allow them to chill.
7. Spread a thin layer of sugar on top of the custard and caramelize with a blowtorch.
8. Serve!

NUTRITION VALUES (PER SERVING)

- Calories: 148
- Fat: 5g
- Carbohydrates: 21g
- Protein: 5g

Conclusion

I would like to thank you for purchasing the book and taking the time for going through the book as well. I do hope that this book has been helpful and you found the information contained within the scriptures useful! Keep in mind that you are not only limited to the recipes provided in this book! Just go ahead and keep on exploring until you create your very own culinary masterpiece!

Stay healthy and stay safe!

© Copyright 2018 – Laura Miller - All rights reserved.

In no way is it legal to reproduce, duplicate, or transmit any part of this document by either electronic means or in printed format. Recording of this publication is strictly prohibited and any storage of this document is not allowed unless with written permission from the publisher. All rights reserved. The information provided herein is stated to be truthful and consistent, in that any liability, in terms of inattention or otherwise, by any usage or abuse of any policies, processes, or directions contained within is the solitary and utter responsibility of the recipient reader. Under no circumstances will any legal responsibility or blame be held against the publisher for any reparation, damages, or monetary loss due to the information herein, either directly or indirectly. Respective authors own all copyrights not held by the publisher.

ISBN: 9781730788581

Legal Notice:

This book is copyright protected. This is only for personal use. You cannot amend, distribute, sell, use, quote or paraphrase any part or the content of this book without the consent of the author or copyright owner. Legal action will be pursued if this is breached.

Disclaimer Notice:

Please note the information contained in this document is for educational and entertainment purposes only. Every attempt has been made to provide accurate, up to date and reliable complete information. No warranties of any kind are expressed or implied. Readers acknowledge that the author is not engaging in the rendering of legal, financial, medical or professional advice. By reading this document, the reader agrees that under no circumstances are we responsible for any losses, direct or indirect, which are incurred as a result of the use of information contained within this document, including, but not limited to, —errors, omissions, or inaccuracies.

Made in the USA
San Bernardino, CA
01 December 2018